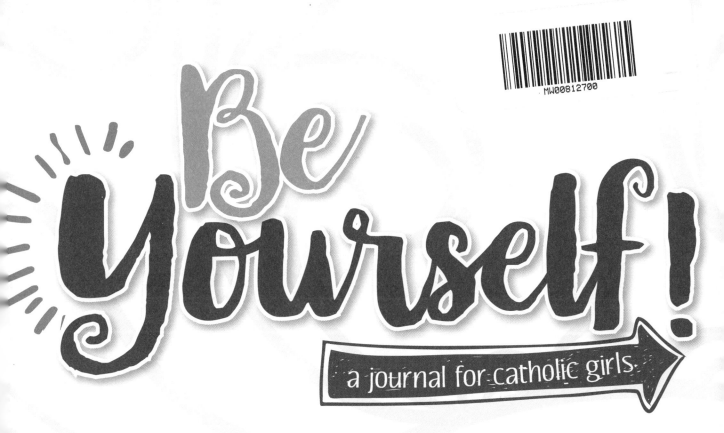

Be Yourself!

a journal for catholic girls

Amy Brooks

saint mary's press

The Saint Mary's Press edition is licensed and published by Saint Mary's Press, Christian Brothers Publications, 702 Terrace Heights, Winona, MN 55987-1320, www.smp.org. Copyright © 2018. All rights reserved. No part of this book may be reproduced by any means without the written permission of the publisher.

Nihil obstat: Rev. Timothy Hall   Imprimatur: †Most Rev. John M. Quinn
              Censor librorum   Bishop of Winona
              May 15, 2017   May 15, 2017

Cover and interior design, composition, and art direction by Laurie Nelson, Agápe Design Studios.
Editing by Jerry Windley-Daoust; design direction by Steve Nagel; copyediting by Karen Carter.

The content in the Saint Mary's Press edition was reviewed and revised by the content engagement team at Saint Mary's Press. Design changes and manufacturing were coordinated by the passionate team of creatives at Saint Mary's Press.

Illustrations of saints for the saint features and the Good Shepherd by Vicki Shuck; all rights reserved.

Additional graphics © iStock, Shutterstock, and Adobe Stock.

The acknowledgments continue at the back of the book.

Amy Brooks and the entire Gracewatch Media publishing team would like to thank the following sponsors of the *Be Yourself!* journal: Generation Life, Charlotte Audrey Anderson, Leah Darrow. Their generosity made this journal possible.

ISBN 978-1-59982-856-5

Printed in the United States of America

5044

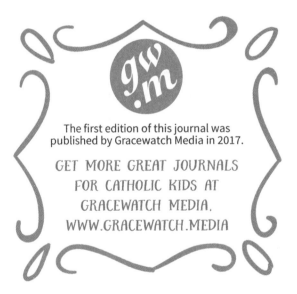

The first edition of this journal was published by Gracewatch Media in 2017.

GET MORE GREAT JOURNALS
FOR CATHOLIC KIDS AT
GRACEWATCH MEDIA.
WWW.GRACEWATCH.MEDIA

HOW TO USE THIS JOURNAL

ANY WAY YOU WANT!

This journal had to be written in such a way that some pages are in the front, others in the middle, and the rest in the back . . . but, you can start wherever you want! Just so you know, the journal is divided into these six sections:

- Who You Really Are
- Love
- Talents and Gifts
- Peace
- Prayer
- Your Life

Some days you may need to go right to the "Prayer" section; other days you may just want to find a page to color. Follow your heart that day, and enjoy your time using this journal.

You can use this journal with *The Catholic Youth Bible* (4th edition) from Saint Mary's Press. At different places in the journal you will find connections to articles in *The Catholic Youth Bible.* Reading these articles will deepen your reflection but they are not required.

JUST BE YOURSELF

As a young woman, I often heard that advice. Sometimes I wondered, "What does that really mean?" Other times I thought, "I don't really know who that is yet."

I came to realize that we discover how to "be ourselves" through our relationship with the God who created us. The same awesome God who knew the universe needed a sun and air also knew the world needed you. How amazing is that?

We truly discover our identity when we nourish our relationship with God and learn his will for our life. This journal is designed to help you enjoy learning about God's will for you.

My personal wish is that you know that God's love for you is so incredibly real! Whatever is going on in your life, remember that God does love you and has a plan full of hope for you.

Every saint who walked the earth had good days and bad days. But the Lord wants you to always hope in the future, to dream big dreams, and to talk to him in prayer and nurture your relationship with him.

The more you nourish your relationship with the Lord, the more you will come to know his will for you. This journal is designed to help you navigate that relationship—on good days and bad days. Enjoy the journey!

May our Lord Jesus bless you abundantly.
Love and prayers,

Amy Brooks

COLOR doodle write CREATE
Make this journal your own! ♡

Let your light shine!

—MATTHEW 5:16

Who You Really Are...

GOD CREATED YOU,
BOTH BODY AND SOUL.

(based on the *Catechism of the
Catholic Church* #382)

GOD
ESTABLISHED YOU
IN HIS FRIENDSHIP.

(based on the *Catechism of the
Catholic Church* #355)

GOD CREATED EVERYTHING FOR
YOU, BUT YOU IN TURN WERE
CREATED TO SERVE AND LOVE
GOD AND TO OFFER ALL
CREATION BACK TO HIM.

(based on the *Catechism of the Catholic Church* #358)

Catholic Youth Bible

Check out the article titled "Being Real"
near Genesis 1:26–27 for more on
celebrating who you are!

GOD CREATED MANKIND IN HIS IMAGE, IN THE IMAGE OF GOD HE CREATED THEM, MALE AND FEMALE HE CREATED THEM.

—GENESIS 1:27

YOUR BEAUTY BASICS

"Do not fear, for I have redeemed you;
I have called you by name; you are mine."
—Isaiah 43:1

Write your full name here.

_____

What does your name mean?

_____

What is your Confirmation name?_____
    (Or what names are you considering to choose for a Confirmation name?)

When were you born? _____

Describe your physical characteristics (hair color, eye color, skin tone, nationality, etc.).

_____

_____

Where do you live?_____

Name two or three activities, sports, or games you enjoy.

_____

_____

_____

Describe your personality in two to three sentences. (What do you wish people knew about you?)

_____

_____

_____

_____

GOD'S CREATION

Look at all of God's creation. It was made for you to enjoy! God created so many wonderful things—from daisies and oceans to the seasons and the sky! What you love most about God's creation may be different from what your parents and peers love most. This is just one aspect of your beauty and uniqueness!

Below is a list of just some aspects of our Lord's creation. Choose your favorites from this list or add your own to come up with your three most favorite aspects of creation. Write them on the lines provided.

RAINBOWS	THE SUN	SNOW	ELEPHANTS	OWLS
MOUNTAINS	OCEANS	RAIN	GIRAFFES	FISH
SUNFLOWERS	RIVERS	WILDFLOWERS	CANYONS	TURTLES
STARS	SUNSETS	CLOUDS	CAVES	ROCKS
THE MOON	DOLPHINS	HORSES	PLANTS	PRECIOUS STONES
ROSES	BIRDS	DOGS	BUTTERFLIES	
MEADOWS	FRUIT TREES	CATS	WATERFALLS	

_____'S TOP THREE !

(write your name above)

1. _____

2. _____

3. _____

Your friendship with God can simply start or be renewed by acknowledging that he made all of creation for you! Think of your "top three" and thank the Lord for creating them. Sometimes a simple prayer is the best!

SHORT PRAYER:

Thank you, Lord God, for creating these amazing things for me to enjoy!

Catholic Youth Bible

For more on how we are called to care for God's creation, see the Challenge titled "Change the World" near Psalm 104:5!

GOD'S CREATION & YOU
YOUR PERSONAL FAVORITES

1. What is your favorite season? _____

_____

2. What flower do you think is the most beautiful? _____

_____

3. Name your favorite land animal. _____

_____

4. What is your favorite fruit or vegetable? _____

_____

5. If you could travel anywhere in the world, where would you go? _____

_____

6. Name a favorite vacation spot for your family. _____

_____

7. Name your favorite sea creature. _____

_____

8. What is your favorite candy? _____

_____

WOULD YOU RATHER...?

God's creation is so incredibly vast and extraordinary that what we enjoy most can vary from what our closest friends and family enjoy the most. Answer these questions quickly—write the first response that comes to mind! Then, ask friends and family the same questions! It's fun to see how some responses will match while others will not! Try making up some "would you rather" questions of your own that make us really think about how much we are able to enjoy God's creation!

WOULD YOU RATHER...

watch the sunrise or sunset? _____

_____

ride a wave or sled down a snow hill? _____

_____

hike in the woods or lie on a beach? _____

_____

go for a run or go for a swim? _____

_____

look at the stars or find shapes in clouds? _____

_____

pick flowers or pick pumpkins? _____

_____

make a snowman or a sand castle? _____

_____

ice skate or ski? _____

_____

make a snow angel or jump in a pile of leaves? _____

_____

go fishing or go scuba diving? _____

_____

climb a mountain or explore a cave? _____

_____

smell a flower or catch a lightning bug? _____

_____

look through a telescope or look through a microscope?

_____

_____

Thank you, Lord, for the beauty of your creation!

SAINT SPOTLIGHT

Name: Catherine of Siena
Where from: Siena, Italy
Nickname: Joy

Advice to others: Be who God meant you to be and you will set the world on fire!

Pet peeve: People being silent about things that matter!

A Letter to You from Saint Catherine of Siena

Dear _____,
(write your name above)

At the age of seventeen, I asked God, "Who am I?"

The Lord revealed to me the answer he would like to reveal to you:

You are the eternal father's daughter. Your eternal father wants you to be humble and grateful and always strive to do his will.

God does NOT want you to label yourself in any other way.

You are NOT the sum of your talents or the troubles you are going through.

You're his daughter, and you were made to serve, love, and offer everything back to him.

Picture yourself sitting on a seesaw with Jesus. From your shoulder hangs a bag the size of Santa's sack. Inside that bag are all the labels you often give yourself or others give you (for example, a good student, a great athlete, a talented musician, a good dresser, a comedian, etc.). While you have that bag, you are weighed down. Now picture yourself giving that bag to Jesus (which is what he wants you to do). Give it to him—all of it.

Now picture what would happen on the seesaw. The weight of all those labels and troubles you are going through—they now weigh down Jesus and allow Jesus to lift you up!

The Lord wants you to depend on him. The Lord wants you to be grateful to him.

It is through that dependence and gratitude that true joy will penetrate your life.

Trust me—look at the nickname my family has given to me!

Love, hugs, and prayers,

Catherine

P.S. If you have any questions, feel free to write back!

Write a letter to Saint Catherine of Siena.

Be who God meant you to be, and you will set the world on fire!

–Saint Catherine of Siena

SHORT PRAYER:
Dear God, help me to be who you meant me to be and set the world ablaze!

Peace

PRAY, HOPE, AND DON'T WORRY!

—Saint Padre Pio

PEACEFULLY DO AT EACH MOMENT WHAT AT THAT MOMENT NEEDS TO BE DONE.

—Saint Katharine Drexel

BUT I SAY TO YOU, LOVE YOUR ENEMIES, AND PRAY FOR THOSE WHO PERSECUTE YOU, THAT YOU MAY BE CHILDREN OF YOUR HEAVENLY FATHER.

—Matthew 5:44–45

Catholic Youth Bible

See the article titled "Shalom: Peace" near Isaiah 32:16–20 for more on how we're called to be people of peace!

BLESSED ARE THE PEACEMAKERS,
FOR THEY WILL BE CALLED
CHILDREN OF GOD.

—MATTHEW 5:9

PEACE

PEACE BE WITH YOU!

SHALOM! PEACE BE WITH YOU!

Shalom is a word similar to aloha! It was a way of greeting people and also a way of saying goodbye in Jesus' time.

Shalom means "peace be with you." When you think of "peace," what do you think of?

_____

_____

_____

_____

_____

_____

_____

_____

_____

_____

_____

_____

_____

_____

TRUTH OR DARE?

TRUTH:

Do you smile at people when you see them? _____

About how many people do you smile at every day? _____

What always makes you smile? _____

_____

_____

_____

How do you make others smile? _____

_____

_____

_____

DARE:

Smile at your parents, teachers, and people you are with—and smile a lot!

The next time you are at Mass, make an extra effort to really wish someone peace—especially someone who is sitting alone or someone you really do not know very well.

Draw a smile! :)

SAINT SPOTLIGHT

Katharine

Name: Saint Katharine Drexel

Where from: Philadelphia, Pennsylvania

Nickname: Kate

Most likely to: Succeed in business

Loves to: Attend formal balls, travel, and help those in need.

Advice to others: Pray for those who are mean to you.

Quote: "If we are faithful in the little, we will obtain grace for the big."

A Letter to You from Saint Katharine Drexel

Dear _____,
(write your name above)

Growing up, I was very fortunate. I was a member of one of the wealthiest families in America. My parents taught my sisters and me that wealth was a gift from God and was meant to be shared.

They also taught us to meet hate with a loving attitude.

When thinking about your life and how to "be yourself," remember: everyone is called to holiness, but our roads look different. We do not all go by the same path. We are called to love. We are called to bring God's peacefulness into the world.

Dream about your future with hope, and keep your heart open.

I once thought I would get married or become a cloistered nun. But when I asked the pope to send missionaries to the Native Americans and African Americans, I was shocked to hear his reply: "Why not, my child, yourself become a missionary?"

So, eventually, I did just that.

But I ask you not to worry too much about the future.

Today, simply ask yourself, "How can I show a loving attitude?"

Pray for everyone—especially for the people you have a hard time liking.

Always keep Christ in your heart, and receive the Eucharist frequently.

Do good work, but be quiet about your charitable acts.

Most importantly, "Peacefully do at each moment what at that moment needs to be done."

Love and prayers, Mother Katharine

THINK AND REFLECT

What was the last thing you shared? With whom did you share it?

_____

_____

_____

_____

Who in your family is in need? What does he or she need?

_____

_____

_____

_____

Who in your community is in need? What does he or she need?

_____

_____

_____

_____

When was the last time you needed something? Who provided it for you?

_____

_____

_____

_____

PEACE LIST

PEACEFUL PLACES YOU HAVE BEEN:

_____
_____
_____
_____

PEACEFUL SONGS YOU HAVE HEARD:

_____
_____
_____
_____

PEACEFUL PEOPLE YOU KNOW:

_____
_____
_____
_____

PEACEFUL COLORS:

_____
_____
_____

PEACEFUL SOUNDS:

_____
_____
_____

Lord, make me an instrument of your peace.

Where there is hatred, let me sow love.

(FROM THE "PEACE PRAYER OF ST. FRANCIS")

LETTER TO JESUS

Complete this letter to Jesus. Add whatever comes to mind and what is in your heart. Sign the letter with your best signature.

Dear Jesus,

I noticed hatred when _____

_____

_____

_____

_____

I feel I can bring peace by _____

_____

_____

_____

_____

I feel like others could bring peace by _____

_____

_____

_____

_____

Lord, help me to know how to be a peacemaker and when to act.

Love,

_____

WHILE YOU WERE OUT...

After reading each "text," choose one verse to copy below. Decorate the space around it with colored pencils, markers, crayons, stamps, washi tape, and/or stickers.

While you were out, heaven sent you a few texts. Check your ~~cell~~ Bible.

Matthew 22:37
Proverbs 3:5
Colossians 3:12–13

GO HOME & LOVE YOUR FAMILY

List the names of your family members.

_____

_____

_____

_____

_____

Describe ways you can show each member of your family love.

_____

_____

_____

_____

_____

_____

_____

_____

_____

_____

_____

Catholic Youth Bible

Check out the article titled "We Are Family" near Colossians 3:18–4:1 for more about the gift of families!

Peace BEGINS WITH a smile

—SAINT TERESA OF CALCUTTA

SMILE CHALLENGE

THERE WAS AT THAT TIME A CERTAIN NUN WHO MANAGED TO IRRITATE ME IN EVERYTHING SHE DID.

—Saint Thérèse of Lisieux

Saint Thérèse desired to love Jesus with her whole heart; but Saint Thérèse also lived in the real world—where people can be annoying! Can you think of someone who "gets on your nerves"?

Saint Thérèse lived at Carmel with a particular nun who, as she stated, "managed to irritate" her with everything that she did. But Saint Thérèse recalled the words of Jesus:

> "And if you do good to those who do good to you, what credit is that to you? Even sinners do the same....But rather, love your enemies and do good to them, and lend expecting nothing back;... Be merciful, just as [also] your Father is merciful."   —Luke 6:33, 35, 36

So in remembering this directive from Jesus, Thérèse set out to treat this "irritating nun" as though she loved her more than anyone else!

Thérèse wrote about her experience in her autobiography, saying, "I tried to do everything I possibly could for her, and when tempted to answer her sharply, I hastened to give her a friendly smile and talk about something else."

This was done with a sincere heart. It was noticed so much so by the annoying nun that she asked Saint Thérèse once, "What do you find so attractive in me? Whenever we meet, you give me such a gracious smile."

YOUR MISSION:

For the next two weeks, make an effort to sincerely smile at someone you don't often feel at peace with. After two weeks has passed, come back and write a paragraph describing your experience.

Today's date: _____   The date two weeks from today: _____

_____
_____
_____
_____
_____
_____

SHORT PRAYER:

Lord, make me an instrument of your peace. Where there is hatred, let me sow love.

Catholic Youth Bible

See the Challenge near Luke 6:27–28 for more on loving those who we struggle with.

FEELING AT PEACE

We often feel at peace when we are listening to a song that we love! Speaking of songs, what is your favorite:

SLOW SONG:

_____

_____

FAST SONG:

_____

_____

SONG FROM A MOVIE:

_____

_____

DANCE SONG:

_____

_____

COUNTRY SONG:

_____

_____

TOP 40 SONG:

_____

_____

CHURCH SONG OR HYMN:

_____

_____

CHRISTIAN SONG:

_____

_____

"OLD" SONG:

_____

_____

"NEW" SONG:

_____

_____

BOY BAND SONG:

_____

_____

BROADWAY MUSICAL SONG:

_____

_____

HIP-HOP OR RAP SONG:

_____

_____

ALTERNATIVE SONG:

_____

_____

INSTRUMENTAL SONG:

_____

_____

SONG WITHOUT A CATEGORY:

_____

_____

Love

GOD PUT US IN THE WORLD TO KNOW, TO LOVE, AND TO SERVE HIM, AND SO TO COME TO PARADISE.

(Catechism of the Catholic Church #1721)

LOVE IS PATIENT. LOVE IS KIND. IT IS NOT JEALOUS. [LOVE] IS NOT POMPOUS. IT IS NOT INFLATED. IT IS NOT RUDE. IT DOES NOT SEEK ITS OWN INTERESTS. IT IS NOT QUICK-TEMPERED. IT DOES NOT BROOD OVER INJURY. IT DOES NOT REJOICE OVER WRONGDOING BUT REJOICES WITH THE TRUTH. IT BEARS ALL THINGS. BELIEVES ALL THINGS. HOPES ALL THINGS. ENDURES ALL THINGS.

—1 Corinthians 13:4–7

[JESUS] SAID TO HIM, "YOU SHALL LOVE THE LORD, YOUR GOD, WITH ALL YOUR HEART, WITH ALL YOUR SOUL, AND WITH ALL YOUR MIND. THIS IS THE GREATEST AND THE FIRST COMMANDMENT. THE SECOND IS LIKE IT: YOU SHALL LOVE YOUR NEIGHBOR AS YOURSELF."

—MATTHEW 22:37-39

Catholic Youth Bible

Check out the article titled
"Understanding Love" near 1 John 4:7–21!

LOVE LIST

Read the list on the left side of the page, which gives examples of ways people show kindness to others. On the right side of the page, list ten ways you can show kindness. Feel free to copy some of the ideas on the right, and list some of your own ideas as well!

Open the door for someone.

Wash the dishes without being asked.

Talk to a classmate who seems shy.

Play with a younger sibling.

Hug your mom.

Listen to someone without interrupting him or her.

Tell someone that he or she looks nice today.

Say thank you to a teacher or parent for no particular reason.

Call your grandparents, and ask them how they are doing.

Say "You did great!" to a peer or teammate.

Collect some of your clothes or books to donate to a charity.

Write a letter to your parents that describes how much you appreciate them.

Clean a room in your house, and do it joyfully.

Compliment a sibling.

Ask your parents what you could do for them today, and do it without complaining.

Talk to someone on social media who seems "lonely" there.

Think of a person who seems to always want your attention, but you would rather not talk to him or her. Give that person five minutes of your undivided attention today.

Smile more.

Give up screen time today, and each time you think you want to look at a screen, say an "Our Father" instead. Our Lord wants our attention and kindness, too.

THINK, REFLECT, WRITE

DESCRIBE A TIME WHEN SOMEONE WAS PATIENT WITH YOU.

_____
_____
_____
_____
_____
_____

WITH WHOM DO YOU NEED TO BE MORE PATIENT? HOW CAN YOU SHOW
HIM OR HER PATIENCE?

_____
_____
_____
_____
_____

WHO IS THE MOST PATIENT PERSON YOU KNOW? DESCRIBE THAT PERSON IN DETAIL.

_____
_____
_____
_____

Catholic Youth Bible

To read more about patience in our spiritual
life, see the article titled "Right Now!"
near Habakkuk 2:3!

IT'S A LOVE THING

We often say we *love* things. What are some things you have said you *love?* Write the names of five or more of those things in the heart below. Then, write the names of the people you love inside the heart.

Try to imagine feeling all of the love you have for all of these people and things in one second. Now multiply that feeling times a million. That's not even close to how much God loves you for all eternity!

"What eye has not seen, and ear has not heard, and what has not entered the human heart, what God has prepared for those who love him."
—1 Corinthians 2:9

Dear _____,

I love you more.

x o x o x,

Your eternal Father, and the Son, and the Holy Spirit

LOVE COLLAGE

On this page, paste pictures of you with people you love around the quote. Use both old and recent pictures. Have fun making a collage of photographs! Try to cover the entire page with photos—but don't cover the quote!

*Never worry about numbers.
Help one person at a time
and always start with
the person nearest you.*

—Saint Teresa of Calcutta

THINK, REFLECT, WRITE

Saint John Paul II once said, "There is no place for selfishness—and no place for fear! Do not be afraid, then, when love makes demands. Do not be afraid when love requires sacrifice."

LIST SOME ACTIONS THAT ARE EASY WAYS TO SHOW LOVE.

_____

_____

_____

_____

WHAT ARE SOME WAYS YOU SHOW YOUR PARENTS YOU LOVE THEM?

_____

_____

_____

_____

WHAT CHORES OR RESPONSIBILITIES DO YOU HAVE THAT REQUIRE SACRIFICE?

_____

_____

_____

_____

DESCRIBE TIMES WHEN YOU FEEL LOVING IS A CHALLENGE OR DIFFICULT?

_____

_____

_____

Catholic Youth Bible

See the Challenge near 1 John 3:17–18 for actions you can take to show more love!

SAINT SPOTLIGHT

Thérèse

Name: Saint Thérèse of the Child Jesus
Where from: Lisieux, France

Loves: Snow
Quote: "I will let fall from heaven a shower of roses."

A Letter to You from Saint Thérèse!

Dear _____,
(write your name above)

I don't know about you, but I like to keep things simple.

I want to tell you that God loves you. Trust me, he does.

I want you to stop putting so much pressure on yourself. Maybe someday you will find the cure for cancer or stop everyone from fighting, but today— today just be truly kind to someone who is, honestly, annoying.

What matters in life are not great deeds, but great love.

I want to tell you something I once told my sister Celine in a letter. There were plenty of times in my life when I wanted to say nothing or I simply wanted to look annoyed!!! There were times when I did not want to pray! There were times in my life that I felt incapable of practicing virtue! It was in those moments (when I wanted to say nothing or simply wanted to look annoyed) that I simply gave a smile or a friendly word!

There were plenty of times when I felt like there was nothing I could do to please Jesus. In those moments, I simply told Jesus that I loved him.

Tell Jesus you love him frequently.

If you need help with something, ask me. I have always wanted to spend my heaven doing good on earth. Let me send you a rose or two. Honestly, it's quite fun letting them fall down from heaven!

Remember—love the Lord with all your heart!

May the peace of Christ be with you—always!

Love, Thérèse

The splendor of the rose and the whiteness
of the lily do not rob the little violet of its scent
nor the daisy of its simple charm.
If every tiny flower wanted to be a rose,
spring would lose its loveliness.

—Saint Thérèse of Lisieux

My Novena Rose Prayer

A novena is a prayer that is prayed for nine days in a row. Here's one to pray to St. Thérèse:

O little Thérèse of the Child Jesus,
please pick for me a rose from the heavenly gardens
and send it to me as a message of love.
O little Flower of Jesus, ask God today to grant
the favors I now place with confidence in your hands:

(Write down your request.)

_____

_____

_____

_____

_____

_____

St. Thérèse, help me to always believe as you did,
in God's great love for me, so that I might imitate
your "Little Way" each day. Amen.

TO DO LIST: LOVE

Circle or put hearts around the ways you intend to show love this week. Add your own ideas below!

Do an extra chore.

Talk to a shy peer.

Smile at people more.

Offer to help your parent.

Give up screen time, and replace it with prayer.

Listen to someone who talks a lot.

Mail or write someone a card/letter.

Hug more.

Play with a younger sibling/child.

Compliment someone whom you do not often compliment.

Encourage someone who feels frustrated.

Make someone feel included.

Say thank you more.

Give up a snack as a sacrifice to the Lord.

Complain less.

the fruit of the Spirit
is love, joy, peace,
patience, kindness,
generosity,
faithfulness,
gentleness, and
self-control.

—Galatians 5:22

Prayer

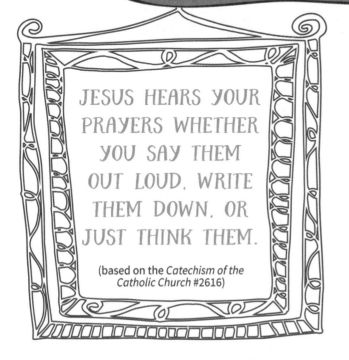

JESUS HEARS YOUR PRAYERS WHETHER YOU SAY THEM OUT LOUD, WRITE THEM DOWN, OR JUST THINK THEM.

(based on the *Catechism of the Catholic Church* #2616)

PRAYER COMES FROM YOUR HEART.

(based on the *Catechism of the Catholic Church* #2562)

HE SAID TO THEM, "WHEN YOU PRAY, SAY: FATHER, HALLOWED BE YOUR NAME, YOUR KINGDOM COME. GIVE US EACH DAY OUR DAILY BREAD AND FORGIVE US OUR SINS FOR WE OURSELVES FORGIVE EVERYONE IN DEBT TO US, AND DO NOT SUBJECT US TO THE FINAL TEST."

—Luke 11: 2–4

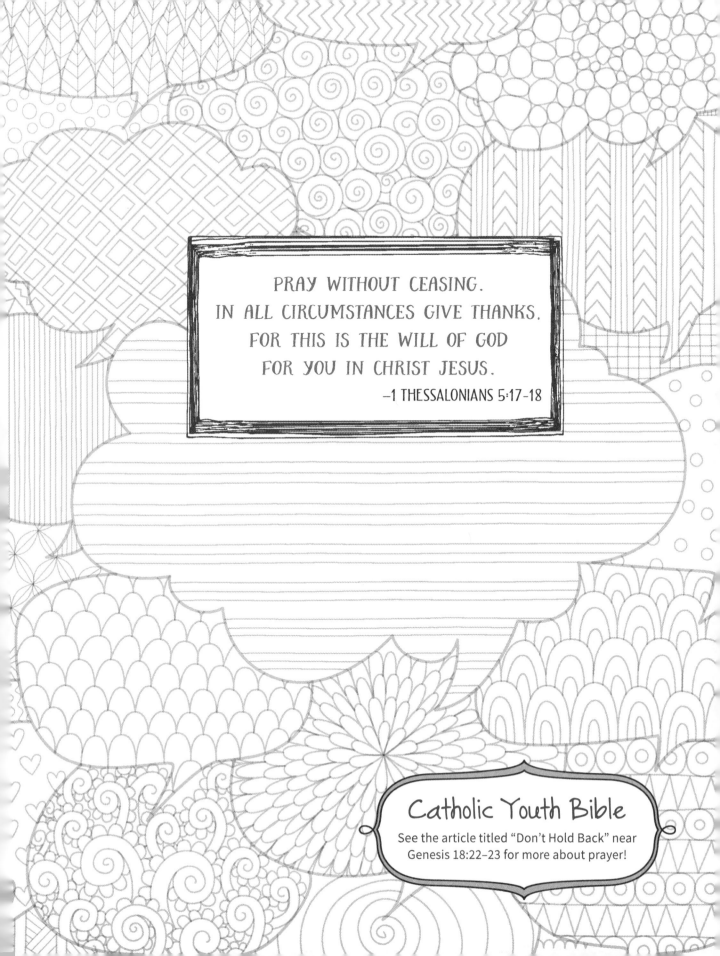

PRAY WITHOUT CEASING.
IN ALL CIRCUMSTANCES GIVE THANKS.
FOR THIS IS THE WILL OF GOD
FOR YOU IN CHRIST JESUS.

–1 THESSALONIANS 5:17-18

Catholic Youth Bible

See the article titled "Don't Hold Back" near Genesis 18:22–23 for more about prayer!

PRESENT PRAYER

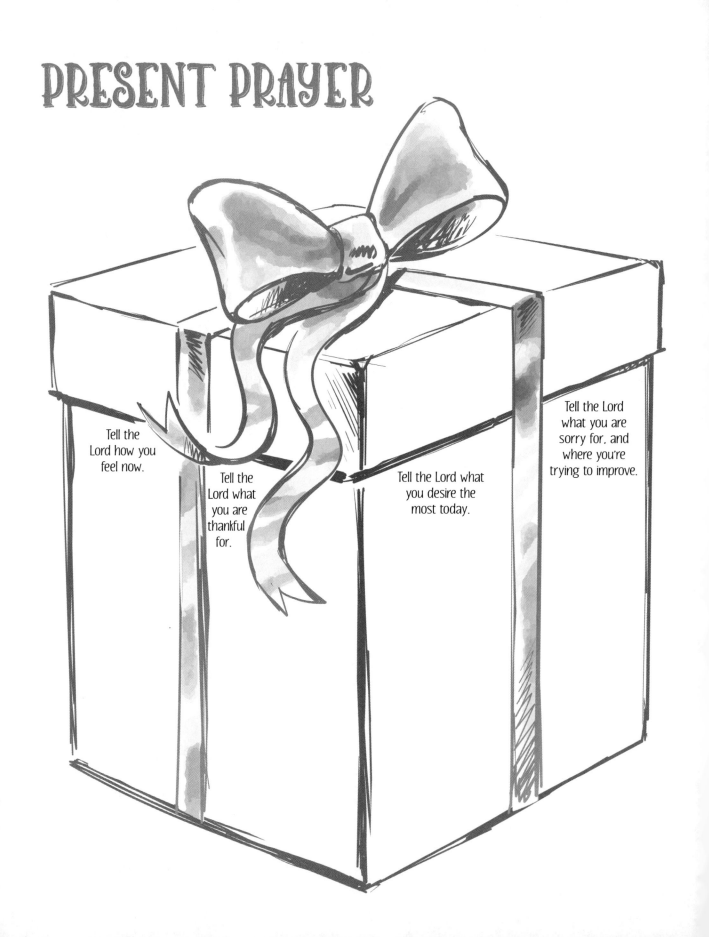

PRAY

Hope

and

DON'T WORRY!

—SAINT PADRE PIO

HOPE LIST

List all the things you hope for—such as what you hope to see, things you hope to do, places you hope to go—anything! Try to write at least fifteen things!

I hope _____

_____

_____

I hope to one day see _____

_____

_____

I hope to one day try _____

_____

_____

I hope to some day travel to _____

_____

_____

_____

I hope to some day see the following changes: _____

_____

_____

_____

My hope for our world is _____

_____

_____

_____

I hope that one day _____

_____

_____

_____

Catholic Youth Bible

See the message about hope near
Romans 5:5 and add some color!

WHAT DO YOU WORRY ABOUT?

Write down your worries. (If you are not worried about anything now, you can come back to this page when you are worried about something, or you can write things you once worried about.) Use your favorite pen for this part.

_____
_____
_____
_____
_____
_____
_____
_____
_____
_____
_____
_____
_____
_____
_____
_____
_____
_____
_____
_____
_____
_____
_____

When you are done writing down your worries, find your favorite highlighter or marker. Now, write over your worries in giant handwriting, "God, I give ALL of this to you!"

Catholic Youth Bible

See the Scripture suggestions for "Worried and Anxious" in the "When I'm Feeling . . ." section near the back of the Bible!

YOUR PRAYER STYLE

Highlight or circle the words or phrases that describe how you, personally, like to pray.
You can circle as many as you would like.

KNEELING

STANDING

SITTING

SINGING

WALKING

WRITING

SILENCE

LISTENING TO A HOMILY

IN A WELL-LIT ROOM

READING SCRIPTURE

PICTURING JESUS
AND TALKING TO HIM

RECITING FORMAL PRAYERS

PRAYING THE ROSARY

LOOKING AT A STATUE

IN CHURCH

IN NATURE

LOOKING AT A STAINED
GLASS WINDOW

DRAWING OR COLORING

GOING TO CONFESSION

THINKING OF ALL THAT YOU
ARE THANKFUL FOR

LISTENING TO MUSIC

PLAYING AN INSTRUMENT

SITTING ON A COMFORTABLE CHAIR

IN BED BEFORE YOU FALL ASLEEP

PRAYING A NOVENA PRAYER

READING A RELIGIOUS BOOK

LOOKING OUT THE WINDOW

PRAYING WITH A FRIEND OR
A FAMILY MEMBER

ADORING THE BLESSED SACRAMENT

Catholic Youth Bible
Check out the article titled "Prayer Types"
near Daniel, chapter 9!

DESIGN YOUR OWN PRAYER ROOM

DECORATING A ROOM IS SO MUCH FUN!

Visualize how you would design and decorate your very own prayer room.
Think about your *prayer style* (from the previous page) and your
design style (favorite colors, lighting, taste in furniture and art, etc.).

Picture what you would want in a room dedicated to praying. Would you want a kneeler, statues (such as of the Blessed Mother), or saint icons and other religious art to hang on the wall? Would you want windows? (One or several? Traditional or stained glass?) Would you like a table or a desk? What essentials would be in the room?

Some ideas to think about are a rosary, a big couch, a big comfy chair, a formal sitting chair, pillows, a Bible, a journal, an iPod with speakers, lights, a chalk board, a big art easel, and a bean bag chair!

Using the next page spread, design your very own prayer room. Use scrapbooking stickers and magazine clippings or draw your own décor!

Want a punching bag in there? Picture a giant bean bag chair, a desk, or a big window?

GO FOR IT! USING YOUR VISION,
DESIGN THE PERFECT PRAYER ROOM!

WRITE A LETTER TO JESUS

Sometimes praying is just like talking to a friend. Write a letter to Jesus. Tell him about your day, your week, what you are looking forward to, and tell him all that you wonder about. Tell him what makes you feel thankful. Tell him anything and everything!

Dear Jesus,

_____

_____

_____

_____

_____

_____

_____

_____

_____

_____

_____

_____

_____

_____

_____

_____

Love,

_____

PRAYING WITH NATURE

In those days [Jesus] departed to the mountain to pray, and he spent the night in prayer to God. —Luke 6:12

We can pray perfectly when we are out in the mountains or on a lake and we feel at one with nature. Nature speaks for us or rather speaks to us. We pray perfectly. —Saint John Paul II

Below, use a pen to write the words of a formal prayer or some lyrics from a Catholic hymn or Christian song. Once you are done writing the words or lyrics, go outside and find some leaves. Bring the leaves in, and put them behind this page. Pick up your favorite color crayon, and make a leaf impression over the prayer(s) by rubbing the side against the paper. Don't stop at one; make as many as you want!

PRAYERS OF GRATITUDE

For the next seven days, write down the things for which you are thankful. Write the date on the first line and use the next lines to name at least three things, people, events, or anything else that you felt gratitude for that day.

1. Date: _____

_____
_____
_____
_____

2. Date: _____

_____
_____
_____
_____

3. Date: _____

_____
_____
_____

4. Date: _____

_____
_____
_____

5. Date: _____

_____
_____
_____
_____

6. Date: _____

_____
_____
_____
_____

7. Date: _____

_____
_____
_____

Catholic Youth Bible

Want some ideas for increasing gratitude in your life? See the Challenge near Ephesians 5:20!

EVERYTHING IS POSSIBLE TO ONE WHO HAS FAITH.

—MARK 9:23

TIME OUT!
LET'S TALK FAVORITES!

NAME YOUR FAVORITE:

Music group: _____

_____

_____

Singer: _____

_____

_____

Actor: _____

_____

_____

Actress: _____

_____

_____

Athlete: _____

_____

_____

Celebrity: _____

_____

_____

Author: _____

_____

_____

SPIRITUAL CHEER!

DEAR GOD,

I think the people I listed are really cool. Please give them strength and the desire to accept and cooperate with your grace, so that through your love, this world will become a happier and more joyful place.

YOUR #1 FAN,

_____

SAINT SPOTLIGHT

Name: Saint Teresa of Calcutta

Name before she entered a religious order: Agnes

Most likely to: Win the Nobel Peace Prize

Always: Carries a Miraculous Medal

Quote: "Give yourself fully to God. He will use you to accomplish great things on the condition that you believe much more in his love than in your own weakness."

A Letter to You from Saint Teresa

Dear _____,
(write your name above)

I want to give you both advice and encouraging words.

First, always remember, before you speak, it is necessary for you to listen, for God speaks in the silence of the heart.

This is true whether you are a teenager, a child, an elderly person, or a young adult.

Love your family. Truly love them. Actively seek to see Jesus in each member of your family, and forgive them. Forgive them over and over again.

Know that your example is worth more than you will ever realize. Whether you believe me or not, everywhere you go, you are setting an example for others. They may be younger than you. They may be older than you. They might not learn anything from you until they see you in action a hundred times. They may learn something from you once and never see you again. Always strive to set the best example. Even if you think no one is watching.

Allow Jesus' light to shine through you!

Find comfort in this: God hears your prayers. Ask him, "Help me, O loving Father, to take whatever you give and give whatever you take with a big smile."

Also remember, God has given you a guardian angel—talk to him, and ask him to protect and guide you. God has given you his Blessed Mother—ask her to help you and pray for you.

Smile, God loves you—and so do I!

Mother Teresa

PRAYING FOR OTHERS

As Christians we are taught to respect, love and pray for all persons. Our prayers are often for people we do not know, including the elderly and the unborn, and for those who face hunger, homelessness, illness, and despair.

Here's one way you can pray for an unborn baby that you don't know. Give the baby a name and write it in here along with today's date as the date adopted. Write in the date nine months from now when the baby would be born. Then use the prayer below to pray for your adopted unborn baby for the next nine months.

Baby's name: _____

Baby's gender: _____

Date adopted: _____

Baby's due date: _____
(nine months after date adopted)

Spiritual Adoption Prayer

Jesus, Mary, and Joseph,
I love you very much.
I beg you to spare the life of

_____,

the unborn baby
that I have spiritually adopted
who is in danger of abortion.

—Archbishop Fulton J. Sheen

Talents and Gifts

CHRIST PROVIDES FOR OUR GROWTH: TO MAKE US GROW TOWARD HIM, OUR HEAD. HE PROVIDES IN HIS BODY, THE CHURCH, THE GIFTS AND ASSISTANCE BY WHICH WE HELP ONE ANOTHER LONG THE WAY OF SALVATION.

(Catechism of the Catholic Church #794)

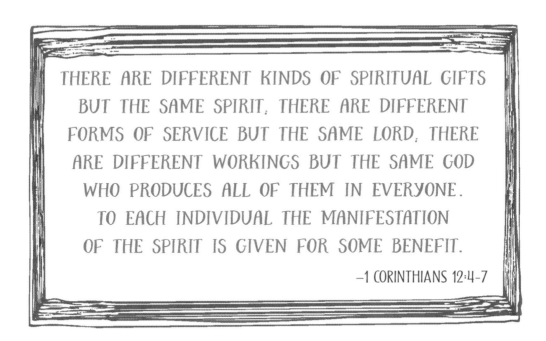

THERE ARE DIFFERENT KINDS OF SPIRITUAL GIFTS BUT THE SAME SPIRIT; THERE ARE DIFFERENT FORMS OF SERVICE BUT THE SAME LORD; THERE ARE DIFFERENT WORKINGS BUT THE SAME GOD WHO PRODUCES ALL OF THEM IN EVERYONE. TO EACH INDIVIDUAL THE MANIFESTATION OF THE SPIRIT IS GIVEN FOR SOME BENEFIT.

—1 CORINTHIANS 12:4-7

Catholic Youth Bible

For more on recognizing gifts in ourselves and others, see the Challenge near 1 Corinthians 12:4–6!

FINDING YOUR GIFTS & TALENTS

TALENTS AND GIFTS
ARE USUALLY THINGS
OR ACTIVITIES
WE ENJOY DOING!

IF YOU LIKE TO
PLAY TENNIS,
DRAW, RUN,
DANCE, ACT,
PLAY BASKETBALL,
SING, WRITE,
OR EVEN READ,
KEEP AT IT!
PRACTICE
AND WORK
TO IMPROVE!

God wants you to enjoy
the gift of life he has given you!

What things would you like to be better at?
Are there things that you have
never done that you'd like to try?

Saint Paul tells us that there are many gifts, but one faith.
Do you ever wonder, "What is my gift or talent?"

List all the things you enjoy doing and the activities in which you
LOVE to participate!

_____

_____

_____

_____

_____

_____

_____

_____

_____

_____

_____

_____

_____

_____

_____

_____

_____

_____

_____

_____

_____

_____

_____

_____

WRITE YOUR OWN NOVENA

If you could spend a day with one of these people, who would you choose?

- Saint Gianna liked to comfort the sick and help them heal, so she became a physician.

- Saint John Paul II enjoyed theater and wanted to be an actor.

- Blessed Pier Giorgio liked to hike, ski, ride horses, and climb mountains.

- Saint Zélie Martin was a talented lace maker and had her own business.

- Saint Catherine of Bologna was a painter.

- Saint John Bosco performed magic tricks to entertain children in his care.

- Saint Thérèse liked to stage plays for her sisters.

- Blessed Chiara Luce Badano liked to swim, play tennis, and mountain climb.

Design a greeting card for the person you selected above! On the opposite page, design the cover and write a note to include inside the card. Tell that saint or blessed why you chose him or her. Ask that saint or blessed to pray for you. Ask specifically that he or she pray for you to find out what your talents and gifts are and that you use them to glorify the Lord!

Once you have written this letter, pray it for nine days. A prayer that is said for nine days is called a novena, which is why this activity is called, "Write Your Own Novena!"

On the ninth day, you can choose to tape a picture over your personal letter, or you can keep it "open" so that you can return to it and read it often. You choose!

Record the date each time you pray. Try your best to pray to this saint for nine days in a row.

SAINT SPOTLIGHT

Elizabeth

Name: Saint Elizabeth of Hungary

Better than the prom queen, she's a REAL PRINCESS!

Most likely to: Give all her pretty dresses away and wear something simple.

Quote: "How could I wear a crown of gold when the Lord bears a crown of thorns and bears it for me?"

A Letter to You from Saint Elizabeth of Hungary.

Dearest _____,
(write your name above)

It always surprises me how many people say to me, "It is so cool that you were a princess!"

I am still a princess—and so are YOU! We are daughters of the King of Heaven!!! There is nothing cooler in the world! I love that we are both princesses and sisters in Christ!

Although I was a princess, your modern world has so much more than I did in my earthly life! But truly, no one has to be a royal to experience the greatest joy in life—the joy of giving! I found so much joy in helping those in need. It did not make many members of my household happy, but I knew that loving God first was my duty, so I risked upsetting others to do his will.

One time I went to give bread to a very hungry soul, but I had to hide it under some clothing. If certain people in the castle saw me, they would have taken the bread from me.

I almost made it, but I was caught! "Whatcha got under there?"

I went to reveal the bread but—it was a miracle! Instead of bread, there were only roses!!! The Lord saved me with a personal miracle! I tried not to look shocked and answered, "Just roses."

I want you to BELIEVE IN MIRACLES!

Yes, you! Truly believe in miracles! Read about miracles in Scripture and stories of saintly intercession. Someday the Lord will allow you to experience a miracle. Until then: Love and give; give and love!

Hugs and prayers, Elizabeth

THINKING ABOUT THE FUTURE

List some cool things you would like to do as a career or vocation! Remember—dream BIG! Have fun with this list! Imagine lots of different possibilities!

TIP: Ask every adult you know what he or she does for a living! There are so many careers out there—one of the ways to learn what they are is to ask people in the working world to describe what they do. You may find something that interests you that you might never have thought of yourself!

_____

_____

_____

_____

_____

_____

_____

_____

_____

_____

_____

_____

_____

_____

_____

_____

_____

_____

_____

_____

_____

Dear God the Father, the Son, and the Holy Spirit,
Help me to WANT to be whatever it is you desire for me!

Love,

_____

I PLEAD WITH YOU

NEVER

EVER GIVE UP ON HOPE.

NEVER DOUBT. NEVER TIRE.

AND NEVER BECOME DISCOURAGED.

BE NOT AFRAID.

She is clothed with strength and dignity, and laughs at the days to come.

– Proverbs 31:25

Feelings

THE PRINCIPAL PASSIONS ARE LOVE AND HATRED, DESIRE AND FEAR, JOY, SADNESS, AND ANGER.

(Catechism of the Catholic Church #1772)

BE HAPPY IN THE MOMENT, THAT'S ENOUGH. EACH MOMENT IS ALL WE NEED, NOT MORE.

—Saint Teresa of Calcutta

EMOTIONS AND FEELINGS CAN BE TAKEN UP IN THE VIRTUES OR PERVERTED BY THE VICES.

(Catechism of the Catholic Church #1774)

THE SECRET OF HAPPINESS IS TO LIVE MOMENT BY MOMENT AND TO THANK GOD FOR ALL HE, IN HIS GOODNESS, SENDS TO US DAY AFTER DAY.

—Saint Gianna Molla

> BUT I SAY TO YOU, LOVE YOUR ENEMIES, AND PRAY FOR THOSE WHO PERSECUTE YOU.
>
> —MATTHEW 5:44

Catholic Youth Bible

To let Scripture guide and support you through the experience of different feelings, see the "When I'm Feeling…" section near the back of the Bible!

HURT FEELINGS

Name some things people have done to you that have really hurt your feelings.

It's okay to write some things down now and come back another time to write more. Sometimes writing things out can help you feel better.

FORGIVING &
ASKING FORGIVENESS

Our faith teaches us to love our enemies and pray for those who persecute us.

If this is difficult for you, YOU ARE NORMAL!

If you find that forgiving comes easy for you, please pray for those who have a hard time forgiving!

Here is a prayer you can say:

> DEAR LORD,
>
> I LOVE YOU VERY MUCH.
>
> PLEASE HELP ALL PEOPLE TO BE MORE FORGIVING.
>
> THANK YOU, LORD, FOR YOUR FORGIVENESS AND MERCY.
>
> AMEN.

Have you ever asked someone to forgive you? If you were to ask someone for forgiveness today, who would it be, and why?

_____

_____

_____

_____

_____

_____

_____

_____

_____

_____

Catholic Youth Bible
Ready to take actions of forgiveness? See the Challenge near Matthew 18:21–22!

SAINT SPOTLIGHT

Name: Saint Maria Goretti

Interests: Sewing, cooking, and watching her baby sister, Teresa

Advice: Stay pure, forgive others no matter what they have done

Favorite flower: The lily

A Letter to You from Saint Maria Goretti.

Dear _____ ,
(write your name above)

If you haven't been told lately, I want to remind you of three truths:

1. You are beautiful. You are beautiful in body AND soul.

2. You are brave, and you have it in you to always be brave.

3. As a Christian, your body is the "temple of the Holy Spirit" (1 Corinthians 6:19–20) and the Spirit of God is truly living in you and among each and every person you see daily.

My mother taught me those truths as a very young child. I made a conscious effort to avoid sin every day. I encourage you to do the same.

If you make a true effort every day to love God above all things, then you are doing exactly what God desires of you.

Make it your responsibility to know what acts are sinful and avoid them. Trust the Lord and the Church's teachings. Know that true freedom comes from doing what is right.

Make loving God and pleasing the Lord a priority every day.

Don't be afraid to love the Lord with all your heart, all your mind, and all your soul.

Be generous with forgiving.

And one last thing, help your parents out; being an adult is tough sometimes.

If you ever need me, I'm in heaven rooting for you! Just pray: "Saint Maria Goretti, pray that God gives me the strength to avoid sin, the willingness to forgive, and the desire to serve my family joyfully. Amen!"

May the love of the Lord fill your heart with joy!

Love, Maria

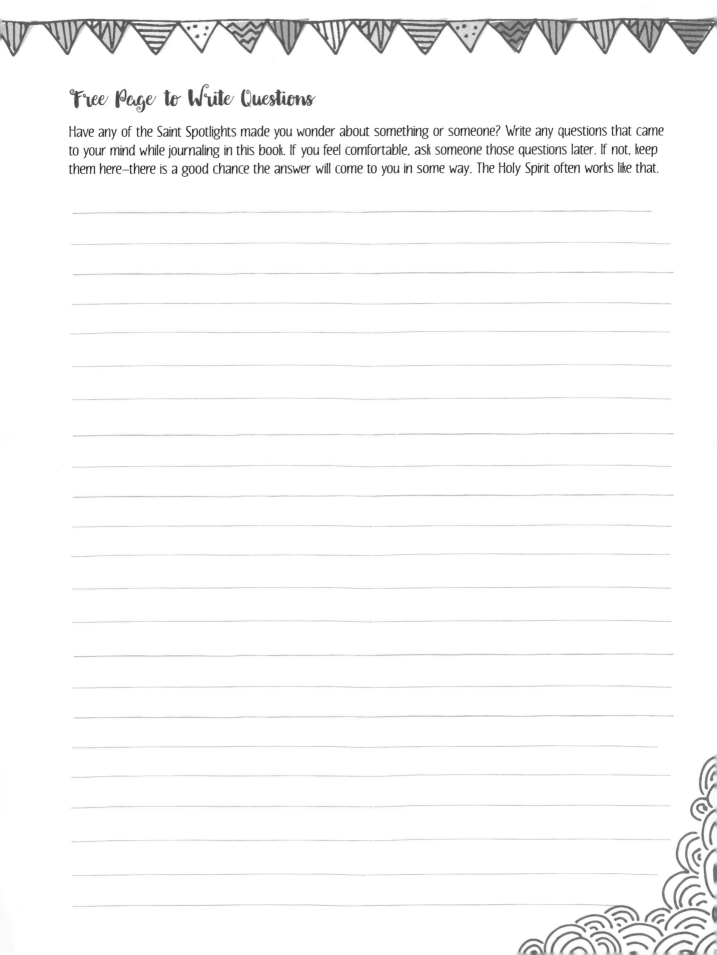

Free Page to Write Questions

Have any of the Saint Spotlights made you wonder about something or someone? Write any questions that came to your mind while journaling in this book. If you feel comfortable, ask someone those questions later. If not, keep them here—there is a good chance the answer will come to you in some way. The Holy Spirit often works like that.

LET'S TALK FAVORITES!

WHAT IS YOUR FAVORITE...

T.V. Show

Book

Movie

Color

Song

Food

Prayer

Saint

App

SHE OPENS HER MOUTH IN WISDOM; KINDLY INSTRUCTION IS ON HER TONGUE.

—PROVERBS 31:26

Your Life

I THANK GOD
FOR EVERY
BREATH I TAKE!

—Gianna Emaneula, daughter
of Saint Gianna Molla

PRESS
FORWARD
AND FEAR
NOTHING.

—Saint Katharine Drexel

ASK JESUS WHAT
HE WANTS OF YOU
AND BE BRAVE.

—Pope Francis

DO NOT WORRY
ABOUT TOMORROW;
TOMORROW WILL TAKE
CARE OF ITSELF.

—Matthew 6:34

I AM CONFIDENT OF THIS, THAT THE ONE WHO BEGAN A GOOD WORK IN YOU WILL CONTINUE TO COMPLETE IT UNTIL THE DAY OF CHRIST JESUS.

–PHILIPPIANS 1:6

Catholic Youth Bible

Check out the article titled "Be Happy!" near Matthew 5:1–12 for more on how to be happy in life!

WHAT DOES ALL THIS HAVE TO DO WITH WHO I AM?

THIS IS JUST YOU BEGINNING TO GET TO KNOW YOURSELF.

Remember, your whole life is a journey of discovery. Every day is actually a part of the trip.

EVERYTHING YOU DO, EVEN THOUGH IT MAY SEEM SMALL, MATTERS.

Keep praying and keep asking God to help you do everything to the best of your ability. He will help you, but he wants you to ask—don't make him feel left out!

YOU ARE AWESOME. YOU ARE VERY IMPORTANT.

Whether you are kicking a soccer ball, running a race, feeding someone who is hungry—or just sitting on the couch, God loves you. God desires you to love him back.

HOW DO I LOVE HIM BACK?

PRAY.

Whether it is reciting an "Our Father" or saying, "Help, I am having a bad day," God loves to hear from you—daily.

FOLLOW HIS COMMANDMENTS.

(And go to Confession when you don't!)

CONTINUE TO SEARCH FOR HIM IN YOUR LIFE.

The Scriptures, priests, religious, teachers, friends, and other Catholics and Christians can help you with this one!

DON'T PANIC!

Keep the faith. Remember, Peter walked on water until he panicked! Have faith that God is there . . . and he will take care of you!

ASK FOR HELP.

Not only can you pray to our Lord, but you can pray to his Blessed Mother as your mother as well. Ask for her help. Pray the rosary. Call on your guardian angel, and ask for his protection and guidance. Ask the saints to intercede for you. Seek help from other prayerful people.

Cut out some pictures of yourself to decorate this page!

JUST FOR FUN: SCAVENGER HUNT

Find the following items, and follow the directions next to each item.

BUBBLEGUM. Get yourself a piece to remind yourself how sweet you are. Tape the wrapper on this page.

BRACELET. Get three short pieces of yarn (your favorite colors), and braid them together. Make them into a circle. Tape it on this page. This is a friendship bracelet to remind you that you always have a friend in Jesus.

BAND—AID. This is for when you get hurt—or when you hurt others. Forgive and be forgiven. Stick the Band-Aid on this page.

LIPSTICK. Make your lips glisten, and remember the beauty of kind words. Kiss this page and leave a cute kiss.

HARD CANDY. Remember to be patient! Tape a piece of hard candy (still in the wrapper) on this page.

STICKERS. Brighten up your day or someone else's! Find a sticker of the sun or a smile. Stick it on this page

A ROCK. Remember the Lord Jesus is your rock and your salvation. Find a small stone, and tape it on this page.

A WORD FROM YOUR BLESSED MOTHER

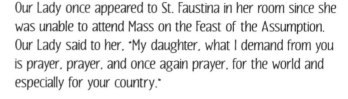

DO WHATEVER
[JESUS] TELLS YOU.

—John 2:5

Our Lady once appeared to St. Faustina in her room since she was unable to attend Mass on the Feast of the Assumption. Our Lady said to her, "My daughter, what I demand from you is prayer, prayer, and once again prayer, for the world and especially for your country."

Say the Rosary everyday, to bring peace to the world and the end of the war. (The Blessed Mother to the children at Fatima)

Have confidence. Do not be afraid. (The Blessed Mother to Saint Catherine Labouré)

Pray for sinners. (The Blessed Mother to Saint Bernadette)

Saint Catherine Labouré was the woman to whom Mary described the design of the Miraculous Medal. During one apparition, Catherine noticed that streaming from the rings on Mary's fingers as she held a globe were many rays of light. Mary explained that the rays symbolize the graces she obtains for those who ask for them. However, some of the gems had no lights leaving them. Mary explained that the rays and graces were available, but did not come because no one had asked for them. Lesson: Ask your Mother!

The Most Blessed Virgin Mary, when the course of her earthly life was completed, was taken up body and soul into the glory of heaven, where she already shares in the glory of her Son's Resurrection, anticipating the resurrection of all members of his Body.
(*Catechism of the Catholic Church* #974)

"We believe that the Holy Mother of God, the new Eve, Mother of the Church, continues in heaven to exercise her maternal role on behalf of the members of Christ."
(Paul VI, *Credo of the People of God* #15)

MARY, MOTHER of JESUS,

PLEASE BE A MOTHER TO ME NOW.

Saint Teresa of Calcutta

A LETTER TO JESUS

Write a letter to Jesus. Talk to him about ANYTHING you would like to discuss.
Remember, he loves you and wants you to go to him with all of your worries and all your joy!

Dear Jesus,

_____

_____

_____

_____

_____

_____

_____

_____

_____

_____

_____

_____

_____

_____

_____

_____

Love,

_____

Most Sacred Heart of Jesus, I place my trust in you.

THE BEGINNING . . .

Life is a journey. You will always be learning more about yourself and working to improve yourself. This is not the end, it is only the beginning. . . .

The first page of each chapter in this book has quotes from the Bible, the *Catechism of the Catholic Church*, and the saints. Choose one or two quotations that you really felt spoke to you. Copy those below, so you can keep them in your heart for reflection and inspiration.

MAKE THE BACK COVER
ALL ABOUT YOU!

MATERIALS:

BLANK PAPER

SCISSORS

MAGAZINES

STICKERS

HOLY CARDS

HOLE PUNCH

SCRAPBOOK PAPER
(DIFFERENT TEXTURES
AND DESIGNS)

PHOTOS OF YOU

WASHI TAPE

CLEAR CONTACT PAPER

WHAT TO DO:

Make a collage!

Use a blank sheet of paper or a piece of scrapbooking paper as your canvas.

Once you are done, glue the entire collage over this back cover, then cover with clear contact paper. If you like, washi tape the border for extra durablilty.

INCLUDE:

- Words that inspire you and describe you

- Pictures from magazines you like

- A holy card that you find inspiring

- Stickers

- Shapes

ABOUT THE AUTHOR

Amy Brooks is a former teacher who is passionate about her faith, history, and adoption. She enjoys hiking, writing, and laughing with friends and family. Amy lives in the Philadelphia area with her husband Matt and three children. She often gives talks about the spiritual adoption prayer and prayer journaling.

ACKNOWLEDGMENTS

Scripture texts in this work are taken from the *New American Bible, revised edition* © 2010, 1991, 1986, 1970 Confraternity of Christian Doctrine, Washington, D.C. and are used by permission of the copyright owner. All Rights Reserved. No part of the *New American Bible* may be reproduced in any form without permission in writing from the copyright owner.

Excerpts from the English translation of the *Catechism of the Catholic Church* for use in the United States of America copyright © 1994 by the United States Catholic Conference, Inc.—Libreria Editrice Vaticana. Used with permission.

The letter from St. Catherine of Siena is based on Knockaert, Andre and Chantal van der Plancke, *15 Days of Prayer with Saint Catherine of Siena.* Hyde Park, NY: New City Press. 2009.

The letter from St. Katharine Drexel is based on Leo Luke Marcello, *15 Days of Prayer with Saint Katharine Drexel.* Hyde Park, NY: New City Press. 2008.

The letter from St. Thérèse of Lisieux is based on Martin, *Thérèse, Story of a Soul: The Autobiography of St. Thérèse of Lisieux.* Rockford, Illinois: Tan Books and Publishers, Inc. 1997.

The letter from St. Maria Goretti is based on Rosica, Fr. Thomas, *"The Life of St. Maria Goretti"* / Salt and Light Catholic Media Foundation." *http://saltandlighttv.org*

The letter from St. Teresa of Calcutta is based on *Quotes and Thoughts from Mother Teresa.* Accessed February 04, 2017. *http://www.livinglifefully.com*

The quote from Gianna Emmanuela Molla is from a personal conversation with the author, July 17, 2016.